THE MONS

A WALKIN

Louise Maskill & Mark Titterton

Photography by Mark Titterton

BRADWELL
BOOKS

Front Cover: Monsal Trail, Chee Dale **Back Cover (l to r):** Congregational Church Little Longstone; Water-cum-Jolly Dale; Haddon Hall

Published by Bradwell Books
9 Orgreave Close Sheffield S13 9NP
Email: books@bradwellbooks.co.uk

British Library Cataloguing in Publication Data: a catalogue record for this book is available from the British Library.

1st Edition

ISBN: 9781910551455

Print – Gomer Press, Llandysul, Ceredigion SA44 4JL
Text by – Louise Maskill and Mark Titterton
Design and typeset by – Mark Titterton
Photography by – Mark Titterton
Photography © Mark Titterton 2018

About the walks

The information in this book has been produced in good faith and is intended as a general guide. Although the maps in this book are based on original Ordnance Survey mapping, walkers are always advised to use a detailed OS map. The best map for these walks is OS Peak District White Peak OL24 1:25 000.

Bradwell Books and the authors have made all reasonable efforts to ensure that the details are correct at the time of publication. Bradwell Books and the authors cannot accept responsibility for any changes that have taken place subsequent to the book being published.

It is the responsibility of individuals undertaking any of the walks listed in this book to exercise due care and consideration for their own health and wellbeing and that of others in their party. The walks in this book are not especially strenuous, but individuals taking part should ensure they are fit and well prepared before setting off.

A good pair of walking books is essential for these walks. It is advisable to take good quality waterproofs, and if undertaking the walks during the winter, take plenty of warm clothing as well. Because the walks will take some time, it would be a good idea to take along some food and drink.

Enjoy walking. Enjoy the Monsal Trail with Bradwell Books!

CONTENTS

Headstone Viaduct with Jubilee Class AJax
Courtesy of D D Brumhead and www.picturethepast.org.uk

Welcome to the Monsal Trail. The walks in this book will guide you along the length of the trail and around many of the surrounding footpaths and bridleways, exploring the area and introducing you to some of the Peak District's most beautiful, tranquil and historic limestone dales.

The Monsal Trail follows an 8.5-mile section of the former Manchester, Buxton, Matlock and Midlands Junction Railway, opened by the Midland Railway in 1863 to link Manchester with London. The line was closed in 1968 and remained derelict for a number of years before being taken over by the Peak District National Park and reopened as a walking route. The recent renovation of the Chee Tor tunnels means that the entire stretch of track is now accessible on foot, by bicycle, wheelchair and pushchair.

Perhaps the most spectacular stretch of the trail is where it crosses the Headstone Viaduct at Monsal Head, but there are equally impressive views at places like Water-cum-Jolly Dale, and the four lit tunnels which have an atmosphere all their own. The trail is easily accessible from Bakewell Station at the south end and Wyedale at the north, as well as from various points along its length. It passes through places such as Hassop, Great Longstone, Monsal Dale, Cressbrook and Litton, and runs close by Haddon Hall and Chatsworth, two of the most beautiful and historic stately homes in England.

Of course, the weather in the Peaks can be changeable and you are advised to take sensible precautions with clothing and footwear. The walks in this book vary in length and difficulty, with location, parking information and detailed notes provided for each walk. Whether you do them all or pick and choose to suit your ability and the weather, this book will provide a detailed and intimate guide to one of the most fascinating and beautiful areas of Derbyshire.

Monsal Dale Station, looking west, 1911. The mouth of Cressbrook Tunnel can be seen in the background
Courtesy of D D Brumhead and www.picturethepast.org.uk

WALK 1 Bakewell Station and the Chatsworth Estate

Introduction (walk instructions on pages 8 & 9)
This walk starts at Bakewell Station, heading away from the Monsal Trail through Manners Wood which marks the boundary between the estates of the Dukes of Devonshire and Rutland. Passing through the wood you cross from the Haddon Estate into Chatsworth Park, a masterpiece of landscape architecture designed by Capability Brown in 1762 at the request of the 4th Duke of Devonshire. Sweeping grassland, woods, ponds, lakes and even waterfalls make this one of the most beautiful country estates in England.

Bakewell Station

The highest points in the walk offer magnificent views across the Chatsworth Estate towards Beeley Moor and Gibbet Moor on the other side of the Derwent Valley. From here there is a clear contrast between the harsh gritstone landscape to the east, with its peat moorlands and relatively few species of plants and animals, and the more mellow limestone country to the west characterised by a patchwork of lush meadows and a much wider variety of flora and fauna.

The walk takes you along a ridge of high ground and over one of the richest Bronze and Iron Age archaeological sites in the area, complete with hut circles, cairns, tombs and rock art. This apparently exposed area was once much more temperate, and it is easy to see why our prehistoric ancestors chose to make it their home. The walk brings you back down through Manners Wood to rejoin the Monsal Trail, from where you can make your way along the trail back to Bakewell Station.

Chatsworth Park

Haddon Hall

WALK 2 Bakewell Station, Haddon Hall and Lathkill Dale

Introduction (walk instructions on pages 10 & 11)

Once again Bakewell Station provides the start and end of this circular walk. Bakewell Station lies high above the town, a relic from the days when the Midland Railway ran services to Manchester. The railway line and the station both closed in the late 1960s, but after a period of dereliction they have been redeveloped and the line now forms the Monsal Trail running for 8½ miles along the Wye Valley.

The track bed is now a green and pleasant route, with many species of plants and trees colonising the industrial workings. This walk takes you past Haddon Hall, the medieval family home of the Vernon and Manners families and the location for the romantic elopement of Dorothy Vernon and John Manners in 1563 during a glittering society ball. The story has inspired many retellings and even an opera, and Haddon Hall continues to draw visitors today. Dorothy and John's descendents became the Dukes of Rutland, who still live in the Hall.

Lathkill Dale

You will also pass through Lathkill Dale, one of Derbyshire's most beautiful and tranquil dales; you may see trout, water voles and dippers in the crystal clear waters of the River Lathkill. However, the dale and the village of Over Haddon, at its head, both have an industrial past that belies their current quiet appearance; look for the soughs and channels of the lead mining that used to take place here, as well as the remains of the pumping house that used to serve Mandale Mine in the dale itself.

The Basics

Distance: 6½ miles / 10.45km (allow 2½-3hrs)

Starting point: Bakewell Station car park, DE45 1GE. Top of Station Road, Bakewell. OS grid reference SK 223690

Parking: Bakewell Station (car park fees apply). There is limited roadside parking near the start of the walk

Path description: Footpaths, tracks, parkland, open pasture and woodland paths. One steep ascent and descent at the start and end of the walk through Manners Wood. Footpaths through Manners Wood can become **boggy and slippery** in places, especially when descending

Nearest refreshments: Tea rooms in Edensor, Chatsworth Garden Centre at Calton Lees

The Walk

1 Walk out of the car park entrance and turn left along **Station Road,** then take the first lane on the left and cross a road bridge over the **Monsal Trail**. After a short distance at the **Station Master's House** turn right onto a public footpath and continue uphill to cross one of the fairways of the **golf course**. Now climb steadily through **Manners Wood** aiming for the top left corner, eventually joining the lane just above the buildings of **Ballcross Farm**.

2 Turn right (ignoring the footpath to your right) and climb up the lane. After a short while the lane levels off to afford a superb 360° panorama of the surrounding area, after which the lane soon begins to descend. Go right on the next obvious track (an unmetalled lane) downhill into **Edensor** village.

3 Walk through **Edensor** and pass the church to reach the entrance gates of the village. Go through a turnstile next to a gate and immediately cross the road to follow a hard footpath leading to **Chatsworth House**.

4 Follow the footpath to reach the balustraded **Chatsworth Bridge**. Cross over the road just before the bridge and bear right to follow the footpath across **Chatsworth Park**, signposted to Beeley and Calton Lees. Head towards a flight of steps in the distance, passing the front of **Chatsworth House** to your left on the opposite side of the river.

5 Climb the steps up the bank and follow the higher of two paths, continuing in the same direction to join the road just before a cattle grid.

Chatsworth House

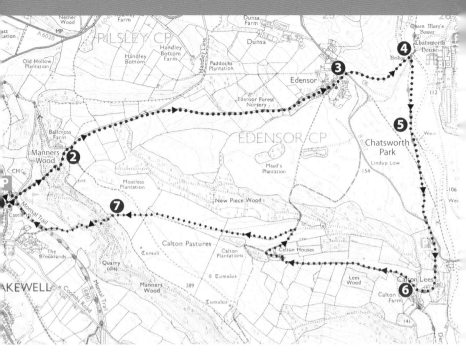

Edensor

6 Follow this track which climbs steadily all the way to **Calton Barn** and house. Walk between the buildings to the end of the track and pass through a gate leading onto open pasture. Turn immediately right after the gate and follow the footpath to an intersection with another track; go left here, following this grassy track to a stile beside a gate. After the gate follow the fence line uphill over open pasture land to reach a gate in the fence on the left. Pass through the gate, and then go through a second gate just to the left of a pond and walk towards Bakewell.

downwards which eventually emerges at the **golf course**. Cross the fairway, following the footpath to go right just before a bridge and walk down onto the **Monsal Trail**. Turn right and walk along the trail back to **Bakewell Station** and the car park.

Cross over the road and go through a gate to follow a footpath beside the road and car park. Pass **Chatsworth Garden Centre** behind a high wall on your left and continue along the road, which shortly bends to the right. Leave the road when it takes a sharp left turn and go straight ahead to a gated public bridleway.

7 Pass to the left of a stand of trees and walk down to a gate in a stone wall leading back into **Manners Wood**. Follow the rocky footpath which descends steeply over a slippery and rocky surface to an intersection with another path, and then keep on the footpath going

9

The Basics

Distance: 8 miles / 12.9km (allow 3¼-4hrs)

Starting point: Bakewell Station car park, DE45 1GE. Top of Station Road, Bakewell. OS grid reference SK 223690

Parking: Bakewell Station (car park fees apply). There is limited roadside parking near the start of the walk

Path description: Paths and tracks with some roads through Over Haddon and Bakewell, including a short road section alongside the busy A6 at Haddon Hall. A steep climb out of Lathkill Dale to Over Haddon. Some stiles

Nearest refreshments: The Lathkill Hotel at Over Haddon

The Walk

Haddon Hall

1 From **Bakewell Station** walk onto the old station platform and go right along the **Monsal Trail**. Leave the trail to the right just before the **Coombs Road viaduct** and descend the embankment to **Coombs Road**.

2 Turn left and immediately right onto a public bridleway. Follow the track until a sign indicating a private no-through-road ahead. At this point, go right through a gate. Follow the public bridleway straight down the meadow, turning left just before a wooden gate. Continue along the public bridleway, passing to the right of a fenced-in veteran ash tree, until you reach a private drive.

3 Go right along the drive for a short distance and take the first footpath on the left. Cross a footbridge and follow the path to join the **Haddon Road** (the A6).

veteran ash tree

4 Turn left along the road, and after 300 yards (just beyond the entrance to **Haddon Hall**) cross the busy road – there is a crossing place for pedestrians from the Haddon Hall visitors' car park. Turn right to reach a public bridleway just past the bus stop.

5 Go through two gates onto the bridleway, and bear slightly right to stay on the public bridleway (ignoring the footpath left to Alport). Climb steadily on the rough track. Leave the track when it bears right and continue to follow the wall on your left to reach a stile at the top of the field. After the stile, walk back towards the wall line and follow it to eventually pass a barn on your left at the top of **Haddon Fields**. Go through the gate straight ahead and stay on the public bridleway, going in the same general direction to reach a gate into a wood.

6 Go through the gate and turn left on the footpath which winds its way down through the wood to **Coalpit Bridge**, an old packhorse bridge over the **River Lathkill**. Continue uphill on the track and turn right where the track intersects another path just below **Raper Lodge**. Follow the footpath to the road.

7 Turn right and walk down the road to cross over **Conksbury Bridge**. Just after the bridge take the first footpath on the left for **Lathkill Dale** and **Over Haddon**. Follow the sealed footpath all the way along to reach **Lathkill Lodge**. Go right up the road which winds steeply uphill into the village of **Over Haddon**.

8 Turn right at **Dale Road** and continue along on the level. Turn right onto **Wellgate Lane** and follow the lane to pass in front of the **Lathkill Hotel**, and then continue to a stile straight ahead just beyond the hotel.

9 Take the footpath on the left, keeping ahead in the same general direction along the high ground to another stile, and then bear left to a wooden stile at the end of a stone wall. After this stile walk slightly to the right across the next field to yet another stile onto a lane.

10 Turn right down the lane to reach a T-junction opposite **Noton Barn Farm**. Turn left at the junction and take the first footpath on the right. Stay on this footpath, going straight down the field with a wall on your right to a gate leading onto **Intake Lane**. Follow this broad rough track which descends all the way back to **Haddon Road** (the A6).

11 Where the lane meets **Haddon Road** at a T-junction, cross immediately over to the pavement on the opposite side of the road and turn left. After about 10 yards take a footpath on the right leading to **Agricultural Way**. Cross the road to a footpath which passes between allotments and buildings, continuing to reach the **recreation ground**. Stay on the footpath through the park, and then with the river on your right walk all the way to the road and cross Bakewell's ancient road bridge. Just after the bridge take a right turn and go up **Station Road**, which climbs back up to the car park at **Bakewell Station**.

WALK 3 Hassop Station, Ashford in the Water and Bakewell

Introduction (walk instructions on pages 16 & 17)

This walk starts from Hassop Station, on the disused railway line between Bakewell and Chatsworth. Opened in 1862, the station saw little passenger use and functioned mainly as a goods yard until it closed in 1964. It has recently been renovated, reopening in 2010 as a charming bookshop, café, gift shop and cycle hire facility, conveniently situated right next to the trail!

Ashford in the Water is a village on the River Wye, and is one of the most attractive villages in the Peak District. It is home to the famous Sheepwash Bridge, a packhorse crossing that used to be a traditional washing point for sheep prior to shearing in the spring. Lambs were penned on one side of the river, and their mothers were driven over the bridge to the other bank, whereupon maternal instinct would prompt them to swim the river back to their offspring.

All Saints Church, Bakewell

The walk brings you back through Bakewell over Holme Bridge, another ancient packhorse crossing over which drovers brought their trains of horses bearing goods for sale in Bakewell market. Indeed, Bakewell is the only market town in the Peak District National Park, and is a bustling centre for tourists as well as locals. The Church of All Saints has dominated the skyline since Saxon times, and Bakewell Bridge dates back to the thirteenth century, although it still carries road traffic into and out of the heart of this beautiful town.

Sheepwash Bridge, Ashford in the Water

WALK 4 Monsal Head, Little Longstone and Great Longstone

Introduction (walk instructions on pages 18 & 19)

This walk starts and finishes at Monsal Head, a renowned beauty spot with stunning views down Monsal Dale and up the Wye Valley. This is also the location of the Monsal Head Hotel, a fine hostelry for refreshments at the start or finish of your walk! Looking down from Monsal Head, the Headstone Viaduct carries the Monsal Trail through the Headstone Tunnel, which was opened to walkers in 2011.

The villages of Little and Great Longstone, along with the tiny hamlet of Rowland, nestle below Longstone Moor, which was largely responsible for the development of the villages because of its lead and mineral deposits and associated mining activity. Footpaths from Little Longstone will take you up onto Longstone Edge, which shelters the village and from where you can look out over the moor. Look out also for the set of stocks in Little Longstone, a relic of local justice in days gone by!

Great Longstone was mentioned in the Domesday Book as Langes Dune, meaning Long Settlement, and is the largest of the three villages. It has the attractive thirteenth century Church of St Giles at its heart, but there are several architecturally important buildings in the village, notably the Shackly Building dating from about 1600, and Longstone Hall, built around 1747 and occupied by the Wright family for many centuries. The Monsal Trail passes through the village via Longstone Station, which closed in 1962. There is a medieval market cross on the village green.

The Headstone Viaduct, Monsal Trail and Monsal Dale viewed from Monsal Head

The Basics

Distance: 6 miles / 9.65km (allow 2½-3hrs)

Starting point: Hassop Station, DE45 1NW. The entrance to the car park is on the roundabout off the B6001 and A6020, about one mile north of Bakewell. OS grid reference: SK 217705

Parking: Hassop Station (car park fees apply)

Path description: Waymarked footpaths with some stiles and short sections on roadside pavements alongside the busy A6020 and A6. A fairly steep ascent through Endcliffe Woods to Bakewell Church

Nearest refreshments: Café at Hassop Station. Pubs and village shop at Ashford in the Water. Numerous pubs and outlets in Bakewell

The Walk

1 From **Hassop Station** car park, walk onto the **Monsal Trail** and turn right. Continue along the trail, exiting on the second public footpath to the right to Rowland and Hassop. Descend on the footpath to the road and turn left, and then at the T-junction with another road go left again and walk under the bridge beneath the trail.

Bakewell's ancient road bridge

2 Bear right towards Ashford, cross the busy **A6020** road and take the private road going uphill. Continue along the road to pass **Churchdale Cottage, Lodge and Farm** on your right, and take the first public footpath on the left (before the gates to **Churchdale Hall**). Shortly afterwards cross a stile on the right into a field.

3 Skirting the landscaped gardens to your right, head towards a stile over a wall and then follow the public footpath across the field which leads into a wood. Continue on the footpath all the way to join the road (the **A6020**). Immediately cross the busy road to a footpath on the opposite side, and turn left towards **Ashford in the Water**.

4 Walk across the road junction for **Ashford in the Water**, turn left and then cross the **A6020** once more

opposite a no-through-road to one side of the cricket ground. Follow this road to where it joins the **A6** (the Bakewell-Buxton road). Turn left, and then take the first public footpath on the left and follow the waymarked path through rolling meadows beside the River Wye. After several gates and stiles the path narrows to pass between buildings and cross a road; continue straight ahead on the path between several more buildings and through a final field to rejoin the **A6**.

5 Turn left on the **A6**. Cross over the road at the first footpath going right, to the side of the car park for the **Deepdale Business Park**, and climb the footpath through **Endcliff Wood** to emerge at a school sports fields. Turn right following the perimeter of the fields to reach a car park. Go right through the entrance of the car park onto the road. Turn left and walk down

Lychgate leading to All Saints Church

the road towards Bakewell. The road bears left and then right, after which take a right turn onto **Church Lane**.

6 Ignore a squeeze stile on your left and take the next left turn into the **All Saints Church** through a stone

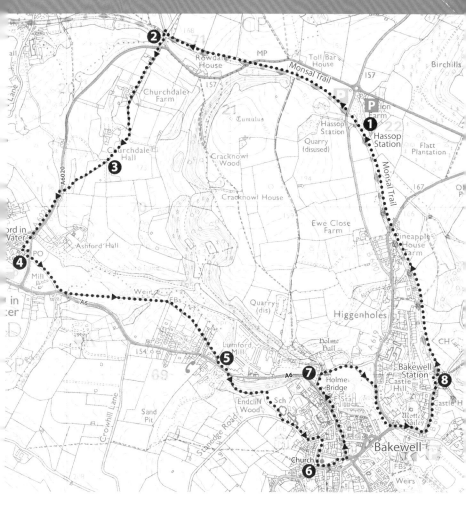

lychgate. Follow the path down and leave the churchyard on the left side down some steps onto the road. Turn right and follow the road to the junction with the **A6** (on a bend) and turn left to follow the **A6**. Cross the road opposite **Victoria Mill** and continue along the **A6**. Turn right at the next narrow no-through-road onto the public bridleway leading to **Holme Bridge**.

7 Cross the bridge and then turn right at the road and take the next footpath on the right. Walk through the riverside meadows known as **Scott's**

Garden. Ignore a flight of steps to the left and go through a gate on the right towards Bakewell's ancient road bridge. Leave the meadows by the left of the two gates just beside the bridge. Immediately cross the **A6** on a bend in the road by the memorial, and take **Station Road** directly uphill to the **Monsal Trail** at **Bakewell Station**.

8 Turn right into the car park at the station, walk onto the **Monsal Trail** and turn left. Follow the trail for roughly a mile back to **Hassop Station** car park.

Scott's Garden, Bakewell

17

The Basics

Distance: 5¼ miles / 8.45km (allow 2-2½)

Starting point: Monsal Head, DE45 1NL. On the B6465. Ordnance Survey grid reference SK 185715

Parking: Monsal Head long stay car park, to the rear of the Monsal Head Hotel (car park fees apply). There is a limited amount of roadside parking near the start of the walk, just by the turn-off from the B6465 road to Little Longstone

Path description: Footpaths and tracks with some sections of roadside walking, mostly at the start and end of the walk. Mostly undulating. Fields can become boggy in places after heavy rain

Nearest refreshments: Pub and café at Monsal Head. Ice cream van at Monsal Head during peak visiting times. Pubs in Great and Little Longstone

Packhorse Inn, Little Longstone

The Walk

1 Turn left out of the car park entrance and take the road to the right that leads to Great Longstone. Walk into the village of **Little Longstone**, passing the **Congregational Church** and the **Packhorse Inn** on your left.

2 Leave the road to the right at an **Ashford and Monsal Trail** footpath sign. Go over the stile to the left of a gate and take the left footpath (ignoring the path to the Monsal Trail) to climb the grassy pasture towards a wood. Go through two gates enclosing a narrow strip of woodland into the next field. Walk across the field, following the waymarked footpath sign to a stile. Cross a track and continue following the footpath across several more fields to reach a lane in **Great Longstone**.

3 Cross straight over the road and follow the footpath ahead. Turn left in front of a low stone wall just before a stile into the **recreation area**. Follow the wall to a narrow (and not obvious) footpath between buildings, which brings you to **Main Street** in **Great Longstone** with the **White Lion Pub** to your left.

4 Cross the road and go up **Church Lane**, which is just to the right. At the lych gate leading to **St Giles Church**, turn right through a similar gate into the graveyard to reach a concession path avoiding the road. Turn left and follow the path, which rejoins the lane again just after it bends to the right.

5 Turn right on the lane. In a short distance, just after **Church Croft** turn left onto a track. Go through the first squeeze stile on the right and cut the corner of a field to another track. Turn right and follow the track until it bears sharp left, and then go straight ahead through a squeeze stile onto a footpath. Continue following the undulating footpath in the same general direction through numerous fields and stiles. After roughly half a mile the path reaches a lane on the outskirts of **Rowland**.

6 Turn right at the lane and walk to a T-junction with the main road. Turn left at the junction and take the footpath on the opposite side of the road, which runs to the right side of a high stone wall enclosing **Hassop**

St Giles Church, Great Longstone

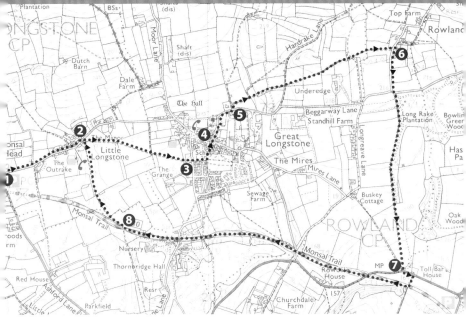

Park. Keep on the footpath beside the wall for roughly half a mile. When **Toll Bar House** and the road come into view in the distance below, walk straight ahead and away from the wall towards a farm gate on the road (to the right of the toll house).

7 Go over a stile and cross the road to the pavement opposite. Turn left and walk towards **Toll Bar House**. Take the footpath on the right opposite the toll house that leads up and onto the **Monsal Trail**. Turn right on the trail and keep going along for roughly a mile to the former station for **Great Longstone**, with its platforms intact.

8 Continue on along the trail. Turn right at a footpath sign for **Monsal Head via Little Longstone**. Turn left and follow the footpath down to a gate, and then continue on the path which rises gently towards **Little Longstone**, where it eventually rejoins the road at the fork in the path that you passed earlier (see **instruction 2** above). From here retrace your steps back to the **Monsal Head** car park.

Former Great Longstone Station on the Monsal Trail

Little Longstone

The view from Monsal Head

WALK 5 Monsal Head and Monsal Dale

Introduction (walk instructions on pages 22 & 23)

This relatively short walk starts once again at Monsal Head. Descending from the viewpoint down the winding path to the Monsal Trail, you will cross the Headstone Viaduct which is one of the most famous parts of this dramatic section of the trail. It featured in many advertisements for the Midland Railway's scenic route through this stunning area, but there was considerable opposition to the railway's construction in the 1860s; writing in 1863, John Ruskin bemoaned the loss of the peace and natural beauty of the dale: "The Valley is gone ... and now every fool in Buxton can be at Bakewell in half an hour, and every fool in Bakewell at Buxton, which you think a lucrative process of exchange – you fools everywhere!"

The heights of Brushfield Hough are a bit of a climb along woodland paths, but this is well worth the effort for the atmospheric views and access to High Dale, should you wish to extend the walk. From Brushfield, descend once again to Lees Bottom, approximately half way between Ashford in the Water and Taddington. Finally you will re-emerge in Monsal Dale, with its limestone geology and huge variety of wildflowers and plants which warrant its status as a Site of Special Scientific Interest.

WALK 6 Tideswell Dale, Miller's Dale and Priestcliffe Lees

Introduction (walk instructions on pages 24 & 25)
This walk will take in geology, industrial archaeology and wildlife. Tideswell Dale was once the site of a quarry, from where dark igneous basalt rock was extracted for use in road construction. However, the ugly quarry workings have been restored and converted into one of the Peak District's first nature trails, and the dale is now a haven for wildflowers, including orchids.

You will also pass Miller's Dale Quarry and the Litton Mill Railway Cutting, also an SSSI, on your way to Litton Mill itself, once the scene of terrible suffering among the children who made up much of its workforce. The peace and tranquillity of the hamlet of Litton today provide a stark contrast to the industrial bleakness of days gone by.

Later in the walk you will encounter the beautiful and peaceful Priestcliffe Lees reserve, an SSSI that is of national importance because of its wildflowers, butterflies, wildlife and geology. If you are lucky you may see several varieties of orchid, and the birdlife to be found here includes year-round residents like woodpeckers and treecreepers, as well as seasonal visitors such as blackcaps, flycatchers and willow warblers.

The Monsal Trail and Miller's Dale

The Basics

Distance: 3½ miles / 5.6km (allow 1¼-1¾hrs)

Starting point: Monsal Head, DE45 1NL. On the n B6465. Ordnance Survey grid reference SK 185715

Parking: Monsal Head long stay car park to the rear of the Monsal Head Hotel (car park fees apply). There is a limited amount of roadside parking near the start of the walk, just by the turn-off from the B6465 road to Little Longstone

Path description: There are some steep ascents and descents in and out of Monsal Dale. Excellent views from above Monsal Dale. Woodland paths with colourful and fragrant flowers in early spring

Nearest Food: Pub and café at Monsal Head. Ice cream van at Monsal Head during peak visiting times

The Walk

Monsal Dale

1 From the long stay car park, walk between the **Stables Bar** and the rear of the **Monsal Head Hotel** to the road. Turn left before the short stay car park and follow the road around to a small semi-circular viewing area which overlooks the **Headstone Viaduct** just past **Hobb's Café**. Go through a narrow gap in the limestone wall to the left. Turn left on the footpath signed to **Ashford and Monsal Dale**. Almost immediately the footpath forks in two; take the right fork (the lower footpath) which traverses the side of **Monsal Dale** through woodland. The path eventually descends to a weir in the bottom of the dale.

2 Continue on the footpath to cross a **footbridge** and then turn left and walk along the bottom of **Monsal Dale** beside the **River Wye**.

3 After approximately three quarters of a mile turn right at a signpost towards **Brushfield Hough**. The footpath climbs fairly steeply through woodland to eventually emerge above the tree line. Go left over a stile in the limestone wall and turn right on the track to walk towards **Brushfield Hough Farm**.

4 Turn left before the farm following the waymarked signs. Go through a gate and turn immediately left just after a derelict farm building. Then turn right and walk along a track, passing a long stone outbuilding and

then a modern barn on your right. Continue along the track to walk beside a high stone wall on your right.

5 When the wall on your right ends, go through a farm gate and leave the track to climb up to the right-hand corner of the field onto another track by a signpost. Turn right on the track towards **Upper Dale**. At two metal gates, take the right gate and continue along the track which affords fine views into and beyond **Monsal Dale**.

6 Walk past a large concrete dew pond to the left of the track and the remains of former nineteenth century leadmining workings at **Putwell Hill**. Just beyond the mineworkings the track begins to descend.

Monsal Head Hotel

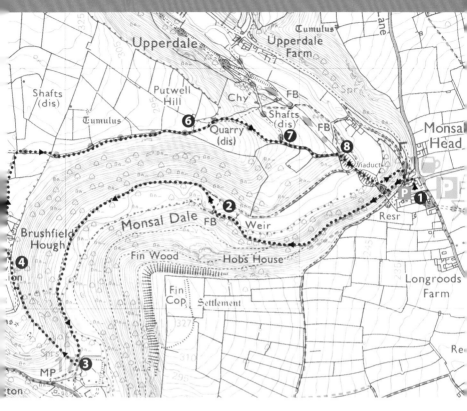

7 Leave the track where it bends ninety degrees to the left and follow the public bridleway straight ahead, which descends all the way to the **Monsal Trail**.

8 Turn right along the trail and cross over the viaduct. Take the footpath to the left just before the tunnel entrance, which climbs all the way back up to **Monsal Head** and the car park.

Wood Anemone – Monsal Dale

The Basics

Distance: 7¾ Miles / 12.5km (allow 3-4hrs)

Starting point: Tideswell Dale car park, SK17 8QH. Along the B6049 off the A623, about one mile from Tideswell. Ordnance Survey grid reference SK 154743

Parking: Tideswell Dale car park (car park fees apply)

Path description: Footpaths and hard paths, with some road walking at Litton Mill and out of Miller's Dale. A fairly exposed high-level footpath along the side of Miller's Dale. A steep ascent and descent to Priestcliffe Lees and another steep ascent out of Miller's Dale. Some stiles

Nearest refreshments: Pub in Miller's Dale

The Walk

1 Walk out of the rear of the car park and follow the hard path through **Tideswell Dale** all the way to emerge at the lane in **Miller's Dale**.

2 Turn left along the lane and walk all the way to **Litton Mill**, a former textile mill that is now private apartments. Walk through the mill complex following the concession footpath, and turn right crossing a stream and then left to follow a hard single-track path through **Miller's Dale**.

3 After three quarters of a mile the footpath narrows and river widens at **Water-cum-Jolly Dale**, where the path can become very boggy (if the path is impassable due to flooding there is an alternative higher route, follow the waymarked signs). Just beyond the impressive limestone cliffs, cross a footbridge and turn right to cross another footbridge by a weir. Climb the footpath to the right, turning left at the top and following the path towards the **Monsal Trail**. Approximately 100 yards before the Monsal Trail where a narrow path joins at an angle from the right, take this path which goes back towards **Cressbrook Mill**.

4 Follow this fairly exposed high-level footpath for approximately a mile, traversing the side of **Miller's**

Water-cum-Jolly Dale

Cressbrook Mill

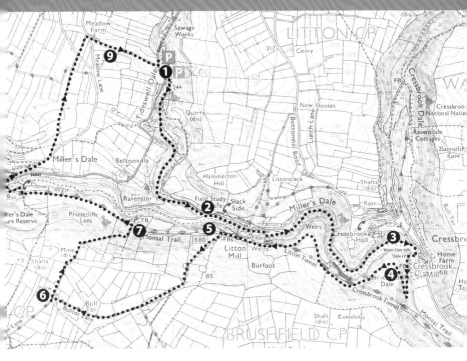

Dale. There are fine views across to **Cressbrook Hall** and into the dale. Ignore a footpath to the right with Litton Mill in view, and continue to finally descend through woodland onto the **Monsal Trail**.

5 Turn left on the **Monsal Trail**. Leave the trail to the left, ascending a flight of steps by the side of an overbridge. At the top of the steps go left towards **Priestcliffe** and climb the footpath up the steep hillside to a gate. Continue climbing to go over a stile in the wall on the right, and then turn immediately left. At the top, turn right and follow the path to the side of the undulating former mine workings, continuing between two walls all the way to a gate leading onto **Bulltor Lane**.

6 Turn right to follow the lane. When the lane bends around to the left, go right up the track towards **Lees Farm**, passing **New Barn** on your right. At **Lees Farm**, go left through the gate into **Priestcliffe Lees Nature**

Early Purple Orchid, Priestcliffe Lees Nature Reserve

Reserve and turn right to take the steep footpath at the back of **Lees Farm**, which descends the hillside all the way to the **Monsal Trail**.

7 Turn left on the **Monsal Trail** towards **Wye Dale**. Leave the trail on the right at a sign to **Miller's Dale** and descend on the footpath to cross a footbridge and reach a lane with a pub to your right. Turn left on the lane,

and then right to ascend several steps to the road (the **B6049**). Cross the road to the pavement opposite and turn right.

8 Turn left up the lane which climbs steeply out of **Miller's Dale**. Stay on the lane to eventually pass the drive to **Monk's Dale Farm**, and leave the lane at the next public footpath on the left. Climb to a gate in the top right corner of the field, and then continue on the footpath in the same general direction. Cross a track and go through a stile in the wall to stiles beyond, leading you across a track and two lanes. At the second lane take the footpath to the right through the buildings at **Meadow Farm**.

9 Once through the farm walk down the field, keeping to the right of a limestone wall. Follow the wall to reach the road (the **B6049**). Cross the road and go left and then right to return to the car park at **Tideswell Dale**.

WALK 7 Tideswell, Monk's Dale and Tideswell Dale

Introduction (walk instructions on pages 28 & 29)

This walk will take you close to one of the most beautiful churches in the Peak District. The fourteenth century Church of St John the Baptist is known as the Cathedral of the Peak, and dominates the village of Tideswell with its graceful lines and classical architecture. It contains many beautiful wood carvings and a number of interesting brasses, and is well worth a diversion to visit.

Monk's Dale is part of the Derbyshire Dales National Nature Reserve, with a wide variety of habitats such as limestone grassland, ash woodland, cliffs, screes and streams. During the summer months the dale is alive with birdsong and bright with wildflowers, but it is a wonderful place to visit at any time of the year. Watch out for the dew ponds which dot the limestone plateau. These were artificially created by farmers to provide water for their cattle, and lined with clay to catch rain before it soaks away through the porous bedrock. They also provide a perfect home for frogs, newts, toads and aquatic insect larvae such as dragonflies.

Miller's Dale, the site of Miller's Dale Station, was once the home of two separate mills, both on the River Wye, as well as a centre for mining and limeworking. The station opened in 1863 to serve the mills and the other local industries, but it also brought increasing tourist traffic from London and Manchester. Again, the peace of the village today belies its busy industrial past.

Tideswell Dale

Former railway cottages, Chee Dale

WALK 8 Wyedale, Monk's Dale and the Chee Tor Tunnels

Introduction (walk instructions on pages 30 & 31)

This walk starts at the Wyedale car park, which is close to Topley Pike and the Deep Dale nature reserve, and also close to the northern end of the Monsal Trail at the Topley Pike junction. You will follow the Pennine Bridleway for part of the walk; this is a 205-mile National Trail running through the Pennine Hills from Derbyshire to Cumbria, allowing riders, walkers and cyclists to experience some of the old drove roads, packhorse routes and ancient bridleways of the north of England.

The village of Wormhill was mentioned in the Domesday book, and it has a tradition of wolf-hunting stretching back to medieval times. It is said that the last wolf in England was killed at Wormhill Hall in the fifteenth century.

The steep slopes and crags of Chee Dale are some of the finest in Derbyshire. The two Chee Tor tunnels, 401 yards and 94 yards long respectively, were constructed to allow the Midland railway line to skirt the base of the 300-foot cliff of Chee Tor, and both tunnels have been opened to walkers in recent years after extensive restoration. The steep cliffs in this part of the Peak District are also popular with climbers, who test their skills against the overhangs and ascents. Some of the cliff faces have bolts drilled into them for carabiners, while others are free-climbed.

The Basics

Distance: 5¾ Miles / 9.25km (allow 2¼-2¾hrs)

Starting point: Tideswell Dale car park, SK17 8QH. Along the B6049 off the A623, about one mile from Tideswell. Ordnance Survey grid reference SK 154743

Parking: Tideswell Dale car park (car park fees apply)

Path description: Tracks and footpaths with some short sections of road walking through Tideswell, Litton Mill, Glebe Farm and Miller's Dale Station. One fairly steep descent into and out of Monk's Dale

Nearest refreshments: Numerous pubs and outlets in Tideswell

Glebe Farm

Sculpture in Tideswell Dale

The Walk

1 From the car park, follow the footpath towards **Tideswell** which runs parallel to the road beside a row of mature beech trees. Go through a gate and follow the concession footpath, avoiding the road. Continue on the footpath to go through the first gate in the wall on the left. Cross the road to the pavement opposite and turn left. Take the next footpath on the right, which turns back towards **Tideswell**. Follow the footpath which leads to a track and then onto **Richard Lane**. Turn right on the lane and walk down to a junction. and then turn left onto the **Buxton Road** in Tideswell.

2 Continue along the roadside until just after the toilets and bus shelter,

and before the bus stop sign go left up **Hardy Lane**. At the road, turn left and take the first footpath on the right opposite **Sunny Bank Lane**. Walk up the right hand side of the next two fields to a stile over a high wall onto a track.

3 Turn left and follow the track for just under half a mile. When the track turns sharp left take the footpath straight ahead. Go through the gate and walk down the field to a stile in the centre of the far wall beside a dew pond. One more field brings you to a stile onto the **Limestone Way**. Turn left and follow the track.

4 When the track bears sharp left, take the public bridleway to the right. Go through the gate and continue on the track which descends all the way to **Monksdale Farm**.

5 Pass through **Monksdale Farm** and turn right onto the **Limestone Way**. Just after a gate, leave the track and take the footpath on the right which zigzags steeply down into

the heavily wooded **Monk's Dale**. Traverse the side of the dale, and at a waymarked fork turn left and descend to cross some stepping stones over the river. Climb out of the dale on the footpath to the left. Above the tree line the path turns sharp right and continues climbing up to the road just below **Glebe Farm**.

6 Turn left down the road and take the next right into the car park of the former **Miller's Dale Station**, and then go left along the **Monsal Trail** towards Bakewell. Pass the remains of the nineteenth century limekilns, behind which is now a nature reserve colonised by lime-loving plants.

7 Leave the trail at a footpath on the left just beyond an overbridge, signed to **Litton Mill**. Descend the path and cross a footbridge to reach the lane.

8 Turn left at the lane and continue past the former mill workers' cottages to take the next track on the right signed to **Tideswell Dale**. The hard footpath climbs gently through Tideswell Dale all the way back to the car park.

Miller's Dale Station

The Basics

Distance: 7½ miles / 12km (allow 3-3¾hrs)

Starting point: Wyedale car park, SK17 9TE. On the A6 south of Buxton.
Ordnance Survey grid reference SK 103724

Parking: Wyedale car park (car park fees apply)

Path description: Footpaths, tracks and short sections of roadside walking. Steep climb out of Chee Dale to Mosley Farm. Care required navigating slippery rocks and occasional fallen trees obstructing the footpath through Monk's Dale. Tunnels on the Monsal Trail

Nearest refreshments: None on the walk

The Walk

1 Walk out of the back of the car park and follow the private road, passing **Topley Pike Wood** on your right. Take the first footpath on the right signed for the walking route of **Monsal Trail**, and ascend the flight of steps onto the trail. Turn right.

2 After a short distance turn left onto the **Pennine Bridleway** for **Wormhill** and descend to cross a footbridge over the **River Wye**. Turn immediately right after the bridge, and where the path forks stay to the left on the **Pennine Bridleway**. Pass beneath a bridge to a gate and then stay on the **Pennine Bridleway** towards **Wormhill**, following the path which zigzags steeply up the side of **Chee Dale**.

3 At the top, go through a gate and turn immediately right towards **Mosley Farm**. Walk part way through the farm and then turn left onto a broad grassy track enclosed between stone walls (the **Pennine Bridleway**). Follow the track, turning right just before a gate at a signpost, and follow the fence line to the lane. Go straight across the lane and then left along the **Pennine Bridleway**.

4 Leave the **Pennine Bridleway** at the next footpath on the right and bear slightly right towards the corner of the field to go between two small upright stones forming a stile in the low wall. Continue down the next field to a wooden gate, and then zigzag down the path into a dale and straight up the other side to a stile. Continue in the same direction up the next field to a stile, and then through two more fields to **Hassop Farm**. Turn right at a track and go between farm buildings to a driveway, and then turn immediately right (just after a barn on the right) and go across a lawn to a wooden gate leading to the road.

5 Turn right and walk down the road passing the driveway of **Wormhill Hall** on your left. Just beyond the driveway take the next footpath on the left which skirts the gardens and then goes to the rear of the buildings at **Chapelsteads Farm** to reach a track. Continue along with the wall on your left to a wooden gate just before the sign indicating 'Private Land', and take the stile on the left. Head towards the left corner of the field to a stile, and then go left towards the corner of the next field and pass through a farm gate on the right onto a track. Just after the track bears left, turn sharp right on the public footpath. Turn immediately right after the next stile, passing a modern farm building on your left. Walk up the field following

Wormhill Hall

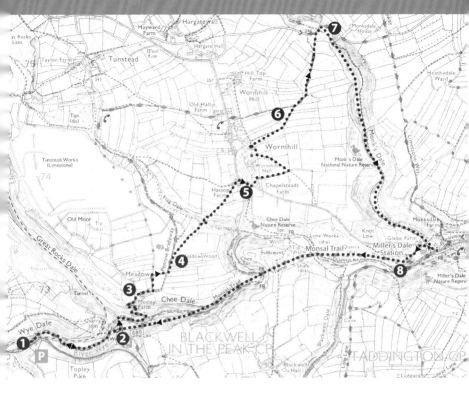

the wall on your left to a gate straight ahead into the next field.

6 Go slightly left across the next field to a gap between two stone walls, and follow the narrow track between two fields. Continue to a stile, and then go right to another narrow wall-enclosed track. Stay on this track which continues down and eventually ends at a field. Follow the footpath all the way down to the road, ignoring the bridleway to the left. Turn right at the road and right again at the bottom of the dale onto the footpath leading into **Monk's Dale**.

Monk's Dale

7 Take care over slippery limestone rocks; this part of Monk's Dale is heavily wooded and there are often fallen branches or trees to navigate. Keep along the lower path for roughly half a mile to eventually emerge from the trees into the open dale. Follow the lower footpath all the way to cross a footbridge. Turn left after the bridge and follow the footpath which eventually begins to climb out of the dale. Above the tree line the path turns sharp right and continues climbing up to the road just below **Glebe Farm**. Turn left down the road and take the next right into the car park of the former **Miller's Dale Station.**

8 Turn right along the **Monsal Trail** towards **Wyedale** and continue for one and three quarter miles through the tunnels cutting through **Chee Tor** to the end of the trail. Retrace your steps from here back to **Wyedale** car park.

Walks for all Ages

Black Country
Cambridgeshire
Carmarthenshire
Cheshire
Chilterns
Cornwall
Dartmoor
Devon
Dorset
County Durham
East Sussex
Essex
Exmoor
Hampshire
Herefordshire
Kent
Lake District
Lancashire
Leicestershire & Rutland
Lincolnshire
Lincolnshire
Greater Manchester
Northamptonshire*
Northumberland
Nottinghamshire
Peak District
Scottish Borders
Snowdonia
Somerset*
Staffordshire
West Sussex
West Yorkshire
North East Wales
Vale of Glamorgan and Bridgend
Wiltshire
Yorkshire Dales
Walks for All Seasons
Lincolnshire
Nottinghamshire
All books are 96 pages and include 20 circular walks
except * which include 19 walks.

Walks for All Seasons

Lincolnshire
Nottinghamshire
All books are 96 pages and include 20 circular walks

Bradwell's Longer Walks

On Dartmoor
The Peak District
The Yorkshire Dales
Walks for All Ages
London
All books are 128 pages and include 20 circular walks

Coming out in 2017

Walks for all Ages
North Yorks Moors
Pembrokeshire
South Downs National Park
Suffolk
All books are 96 pages and include 20 circular walks

Bradwell's Pocket Walking Guides

Essex
Peak District
Somerset
Yorkshire Dales
All books are 48 pages and include 10 circular walks

Bradwell's Walking Guide Buxton

32 pages and includes 8 circular walks in and around Buxton

BRADWELL
BOOKS